QUAKER QUICKS

Hearing the Light

QUAKER QUICKS

Hearing the Light

Rhiannon Grant

CHRISTIAN ALTERNATIVE
BOOKS

Winchester, UK
Washington, USA

JOHN HUNT PUBLISHING

First published by Christian Alternative Books, 2021
Christian Alternative Books is an imprint of John Hunt Publishing Ltd.,
No. 3 East St., Alresford, Hampshire SO24 9EE, UK
office@jhpbooks.com
www.johnhuntpublishing.com
www.christian-alternative.com

For distributor details and how to order please visit the 'Ordering' section on our website.

Text copyright: Rhiannon Grant 2020

ISBN: 978 1 78904 504 8
978 1 78904 505 5 (ebook)
Library of Congress Control Number: 2020940140

A CIP catalogue record for this book is available from the British Library.

Design: Stuart Davies

UK: Printed and bound by CPI Group (UK) Ltd, Croydon, CR0 4YY
Printed in North America by CPI GPS partners

We operate a distinctive and ethical publishing philosophy in
all areas of our business, from our global network of authors to
production and worldwide distribution.

Contents

Previous Titles

Quakers Do What! Why?, Christian Alternative Books, 9781789044058

Theology from Listening: Finding the Core of Liberal Quaker Theological Thought, Brill, 9789004427334

Between Boat and Shore, Manifold Press, 9781908312679

Telling the Truth about God, Christian Alternative Books, 9781789040814

British Quakers and Religious Language, Brill, 9789789004379

Acknowledgements

This book is dedicated to the glory of God.

I was able to write this book thanks to a grant from the K Blundell Trust, administered by the Society of Authors. I was able to do the research for this book thanks to paid study leave from my employer, Woodbrooke, the Quaker centre in Birmingham, UK. I am very grateful for support from my friends, family, and colleagues, of whom I can only name a few here. Particular thanks to Michael Booth, Nic Burton, Gill Coffin, Taz Cooper, Ben Pink Dandelion, Betty Hagglund, Jon Kershner, Abigail Maxwell, Mackenzie Morgan, Rachel Muers, Tim Pitt-Payne, Christy Randazzo, Judith Roads, Susan Robson, Mark Russ, Janet Scott, Ben Wood, and Stewart Yarlett for conversations during this process – and to everyone at Woodbrooke, colleagues at Britain Yearly Meeting, and the members of Britain Yearly Meeting's Book of Discipline Revision Committee. My partner, Piangfan Angela Naksukpaiboon, has been a wellspring of support and understanding.

What Quakers Know

Quakers know that something – God, the Light, the Spirit, whatever you call it – is available to everyone, within ourselves, and offers us guidance when we are able to accept it.

Quakers know that the kingdom of God – the Divine Commonwealth, heaven on earth, whatever you call it – is a place of peace, a place of equality and justice, and a place of love.

Quakers know that listening to this guidance, attending to the Light Within and following where it calls us, is difficult but can be learned with practice. There are any number of ways in which this process can go wrong, and over time Quakers have put in place some safeguards, which I'll be discussing when I get to 'How We Know'. But the fact of the difficulty itself, and that we need other people around us to help us hear the Light, is part of what we know.

Quakers know that connection and relationship are central to the spiritual life. Quakers know that meeting – as in 'meeting for worship' – is vital and that although individual and solitary prayer and other practices can also be important we are more likely to find the voice of God speaking to us when we are working with a group who all aim to hear God into speech.

In this book, I have chosen to begin with what Quakers know, so that I can talk in detail about how we know and the process by which Quakers find these things out. I talk about knowledge and not belief because I am going to argue that we have evidence, enough evidence to be confident about these claims. Of course, you may disagree – there's material here to construct multiple different plausible positions – and at the end of the book, I'll consider the question of whether or not the evidence I have presented here should convince you. I'll also suggest some ways you can test it for yourself.

I am a Quaker and in this book I talk about the Quaker community using the plural first person, 'we': we know this, we do that, we tend to hedge about with multiple qualifiers about the other. I aim to present evidence for these claims, which are based on experience and research; however, this text has not been tested by any specific Quaker community and all the claims remain my personal responsibility. I address you, the reader, in the second person: you may or may not be a Quaker, you may or may not know much about Quakers, and depending whether or not you find me convincing, you might change your mind about Quakers by the end of the book! I also use the first person when I am speaking solely about myself. If there are mistakes here, those are mine.

The claims I made above, about what Quakers know, will appear repeatedly. They can be phrased in different ways – as I'll discuss in the section on language – but the core themes, of direct contact with the divine, of sensing something which gives guidance, of finding ways to oppose violence and support love and truth, and of working as individuals within community, come up over and over again. They could be split up but frequently, in exploring one, I find that it is connected to another one or to all of them. Mostly, unless some evidence applies to some parts of this and not others, I consider these claims together as the core of Quaker theology.

Having been so bold about what Quakers know I should now say a few things about what Quakers don't know or don't all know. I should also now clarify that in this book I focus on one tradition within Quakerism, often called the liberal Quaker branch, and the weight given to elements in what follows would be different in other Quaker traditions. Within the liberal Quaker tradition, then, some Quakers have a strong experience of God as transcending this world or fully external, and know that to be true for them. Others have a strong experience of God as absent or nonexistent, and know that to be true for them. Some have strong experiences of God as shown in Jesus Christ, others of the divine revealed through other scriptures or traditions, and still others experience all these as potentially useful fictions. Some Quakers have no strong experiences of any of these kinds, and rely on the less dramatic and more everyday experience of participating in the Quaker way. Many change their minds over time. Because Quakerism is a practical faith which takes new evidence into account, we have space to deal with it when people change their minds. We don't always do this well, as a long history of Quaker disagreements and splits reveals, but ideally, Quakers are both open to new experiences and confident in what we have discovered. This is difficult, though, and even when we work hard not to split our community, we sometimes take refuge in uncertainty to avoid conflict or sounding weird – as well as embracing real doubt when it's part of the process.

Observation suggests, however, that we all know that guidance is available through the Quaker method. Our exact experience of this, and the way we describe and interpret the source of that guidance, can differ, but we go on using the method and finding answers which work. Do you know the old joke about the philosopher who spends all day doubting the existence of other minds, then goes home and greets her partner just as if other minds exist? Both the doubt and the practice are real, and I would argue that the philosopher both knows that it's difficult to prove that her partner has a mind, and knows that her partner does have a mind. She doesn't just act as if her partner has a mind, but takes that for granted in everyday interactions. I am a philosopher, and in this book, I am at home and not at work. I know that you have a mind and that the God I experience in meeting for worship is real, and while I present evidence for the second claim, I focus on what works in the ordinary world. Be ready for surprises, though: the God I experience may not be what you expect from the word 'God', and reality might turn out to be more complicated than we thought.

In outline, this book is a discussion of core liberal Quaker theology – the claims with which I began. I start with a few pieces of background information and scene-setting, covering epistemology (the study of how people know). Much of this comes from the wider traditions of philosophy and theology. I also look at Quakers in general, explaining how liberal Quakers may differ from others, and explore liberal Quaker uses of language specifically. Then I move into some detail. First, I look at the key questions: how do Quakers find out theological stuff? Secondly, I look at Quaker process and how we use meeting for worship as a foundation for finding the answers to questions, including practical and theological ones. These are books produced by modern Quaker communities around the world, and I explain what they say and how they relate to – and provide evidence for – the core Quaker claims. Finally, I look at whether I've succeeded and why you might or might not agree with me, and suggest some ways you might explore these questions further.

An Introduction to Knowing

What could anyone possibly know about God, and how? How do people even know obvious things, like that I am a real person and not a brain in a vat plugged into a giant computer?

At the risk of – no, in the certain knowledge that I am – dismissing centuries of philosophical work in a single paragraph, I confess that I have introduced those giant questions without any intention of dealing with them in detail. There's a fun philosophical game which involves inventing scenarios in which the world is not at all as it's usually perceived. There could be an evil demon, a misguided scientist, or a talented philosopher-programmer trapping everyone in a vast and complex mirage (or perhaps just you; maybe I am a figment of the imagination of the powerful figure who rules everything and lies to you and all your senses). Perhaps. But until there is any evidence for this, other than the ability of human minds to imagine many fantastic situations, what anyone actually knows is related to their individual experience and the way in which their community validates that. There is a social element to knowledge. People work together to understand what is happening and describe it. If you speak a different language, you may have different categories, different emphases (on verbs rather than nouns, for example), and other different approaches to the world, like a different understanding of the nature of time. In groups, people can communicate about their experiences and compare them, not exactly but enough to form basic understandings: to find out whose colour vision is different, whose pain is strongest, or who associates shapes with sounds.

For different types of knowledge, different kinds of evidence are required. You can say you know how to ride a bike when you can demonstrate that you can ride a bike – and perhaps even if you can't right now, but you did ride a bike in the past.

You can say that you know where something is if you can find it or give someone else directions to find it. You can say that you know that it's raining if you can feel the rain falling on your head, or if you can see through the window that it's raining, or maybe if you hear a reliable weather forecast on the radio, or if someone trustworthy came in from outside and reported on the weather. You can say that you know someone loves you if they say so and their actions are in line with that claim. You can say that you know that this is your hand just by holding up your hand and using the word 'hand' in the same way as the rest of your community – you have direct knowledge, everyone agrees with you, and the issue of presenting evidence doesn't really come into it. In fact, I very rarely even make the claim 'this is my hand' because it's too obvious to be worth saying; instead, I talk about my hands when something is or might be happening to them: 'My hand hurts.' 'Please hold my hand.'

That being so, for the purposes of this book please let us accept that we can and do know some stuff reasonably well. Bikes get ridden, rain is correctly identified, hands are held. What do we know and not know?

A politician got roundly mocked a few years ago for dividing known and unknown things themselves into knowns and unknowns – but he had a point. There are things we know that we know, things we know we don't know, things we know but don't realise it, and things we don't even know we don't know. In this book I am mainly going to talk about the things which Quakers know – things Quakers know we know and things Quakers know but don't realise it – but in this introduction I want to spend a little while talking about what we don't know: what we know we don't know, and what we don't even know that we don't know.

In case you are already confused, let me start with some very concrete examples of things I know and don't know about Quakers. I know – and I know that I know – some nice simple facts about Quakers. For example, we're a religious group which began in England in the 1650s and has since spread worldwide, with all the diversity that process produces. I know that we worship using silence as a tool to make space to listen. I know about my place as a Quaker within the many Quaker traditions – I'm a liberal Quaker, part of a group which accepts modern ideas about the origins of the Bible and the human species, and practises silent or unprogrammed worship. I'm also heavily involved in some of the processes by which my tradition is both developed and passed on. I also know some stuff which is much harder to put into words: I know what it's like to participate in Quaker worship, I know how Quakers make decisions by trying to find out what is the right way forward rather than what someone wants, and I know more or less what to expect when I attend an unprogrammed Quaker meeting.

I probably know things about Quakers which I don't know that I know. Obviously, I can't give you an example of something I currently don't know that I know, but here's an example of something I knew and didn't realise until someone else said something. Growing up a Quaker, I had always spoken of 'going to meeting' and of 'belonging to a Quaker meeting'. Any word develops its own grammar when it's used by a relatively small group in consistent ways. The first time I heard someone talking about 'going to Quakers' it sounded wrong to me – I understood perfectly well what was meant, but it felt out of place – and I realised that I *knew* how to use the words 'meeting' and 'Quaker' within the grammar of the British Quaker community, without really knowing that I knew. Similarly, when someone else asked whether a person 'belonged to a Quaker meeting house', I knew that was not how it worked, although I could see what was intended and why the mistake would arise. Both 'meeting' and 'meeting house' – community and building – might be covered by the word 'church' in another Christian community. One belongs to a Quaker community, like a Quaker meeting; the community might or might not worship in a meeting house, but if it does, the meeting house belongs to the community and not the other way around.

Similarly, I don't know what I don't know. Living and working mainly in the British context, there are many things about Quakers worldwide which I don't know that I don't know until I make a mistake and someone points it out to me.

And there are vast swaths of stuff which I know I know nothing about. I love history and archaeology but I've never studied history and I know there are things I miss – so there will be very little history in this book, which is concerned with the present and recent past. Nobody knows about the future, or even everything there is to know about another person. The biggest one, though, is knowing about God. If there is any being, energy field, force, sense, deeper level, or person which can be called God, it seems logical to think that we are basically unable to understand anything about that God. Human beings are so different in form from God, and so lacking in direct and repeatable evidence about God, that to claim to know anything about God might be completely absurd. Certainly anything we might say about God would be wrong as well as right, only ever an approximation to roughly shove this amazing and incomprehensible God into something human enough for us to be able to talk about it.

The extraordinary claim I am going to make in this book is that despite that, we can and do know some things about God. I'm going to focus on what Quakers know because that is my own tradition and I can speak from my own experience of Quaker ways as well as drawing on all the many things other Quakers have said. I am clear that other people can also know about the reality I call God – some of them would use that word and others wouldn't – and that some of them do have such knowledge. I argue that this reality is known to us through the experience of presence, and there remains a lot which we cannot know, especially about whether God goes beyond the part we can experience into an external realm. I also think that some people (even some Quakers) are wrong in their impression of God and hold views, apparently based on their knowledge of God, which are harmful to themselves or others. At least some of them probably think the same about me. Some people will also think that what I say here is absurd, and I'm not worried about that – I hope you have a good laugh. Furthermore, I'm very happy to acknowledge that I'm probably mistaken about some things in this book.

However, I have done my best to give my understanding as I have it at the moment, and so if I'm wrong about something, it will of course be something I don't know that I don't know. I am obliged, therefore, to leave identifying those things as an exercise for the reader.

Quakers know that everyone can have access to the love and guidance of God. I believe that, working as a community, we can sort out what is really from God and what is shaped by our prejudices and desires. God leads us to witness to our experience of God and what life in God is like: peaceful, just, equitable, honest, simple, and friendly. Sounds good, but difficult, right? Quaker lives and methods testify to the reality of this possibility.

Light, Listening and other Language

Quakers have a rich collection of ways of talking about faith and spiritual matters. Because of the nature of these topics, many of those ways are metaphorical. We use images, or comparisons, or analogies, or generally try to convey one meaning by means of another. In this section, I want to introduce some of the language I use in this book. I'll also mention some things I don't use, and why. I wrote much more about language for God in a previous book, *Telling the Truth about God* (also in the Quaker Quicks series from Christian Alternative and published in 2019) so here I focus on the issues I need to consider in relation to the content of this book: the questions of theology and spiritual experience.

Light, the Light. Quakers use the word Light a lot – for God, and for God within us. This can be a metaphor drawn from sensory experience, using light to see by. It also has roots in traditional Christian language, especially the Gospel of John, where Jesus Christ is described as the true light. This light, Christ, enters the world and opposes the darkness.

The image, light, can be helpful. Having roots in both a common experience and Christian tradition, it can be easy for many people to relate to. The idea of a light shining into us, showing where we are doing well and where we are making mistakes, can be powerful. Some illustrations – for example, in children's books about Quaker worship – picture the inner light as a candle in someone's chest. It can be visualised, for example, as a glowing light around someone who needs prayer. It can be understood as the inward light, something which shines into our hearts and minds to show up the places which need work, like a torch beam which shows up the cobwebs in the cupboard.

The use of the word 'light' can also be difficult and excluding. Not everyone has the experience of seeing or of a mind's eye, and so 'light' isn't a meaningful metaphor to everyone – if you are blind, or partially sighted in such a way that bright light is painful, it might be an alien or distressing metaphor. 'Light' can also mean 'not heavy' or 'pale skinned'. In the society in which I live, white supremacy is common and often built into our social structures in ways which are hidden, especially from well-meaning white people who don't want to be racist as individuals but benefit from racism embedded in our systems. In that context, putting 'light' as automatically good and 'dark' as automatically bad can reinforce that harmful pattern. Similarly, prejudice against people who are fat means that focusing on 'light' things as better than 'heavy' things can reinforce a harmful pattern.

Problems of this kind are hard to avoid entirely – words in the English language often have lots of meanings, as other examples in this chapter show. I try to use 'Light', often with the capital L, in contexts which make it clear that I am using it a sensory metaphor for the divine. However, these problems encouraged me to try and clarify the metaphorical nature of my use of these words in another way, by mixing my metaphors.

Listening, hearing. Again, for many people this will be an ordinary experience: listening to music, listening to someone talk, hearing a noise. On its own, this could mean that it was easy to take it too literally in this context. Religious people who describe hearing God's voice are often assumed to be hearing voices in the sense of experiencing auditory hallucinations. Some religious people do have that experience, but I don't think it's characteristic of the Quaker experiences which I am describing in this book. It also raises similar issues to those involved in the metaphors of seeing and light: if I only wrote about 'listening', people who are deaf or hard of hearing might find this excluding.

Instead, in the title of this book I chose to use both sensory metaphors: *Hearing the Light.* The phrase 'listen to the light' has been used before, and religious experience often involves multiple senses. In the New Testament book of Acts, Paul's encounter with Jesus on the road to Damascus is told twice (once in Chapter 9 and once in 22), and the details switch – there is both a light and a voice, but it's not clear which is for Paul alone and which is witnessed by the whole group. One way to understand this is to think of both as metaphors for a direct encounter which doesn't actually come through either physical sense.

If I weren't trying to keep my title to a sensible number of words, I could have added other senses. We can also feel the light, taste God's voice, smell the way forward, okay, I don't really hear other Quakers using those! But we could. We do talk about sensing a presence or the feeling of the meeting. Religious experience can come through any of our senses, all of them, or none. It has been suggested that sensing God is actually another sense, beyond the ordinary. Whether that's true or not, it is the case that sensing God is not a single experience.

Within. I have already used this word several times, and Quakers like to use it to emphasise the directness of our connection to the divine. The Light within. Christ within. That of God within. 'Within' is also a metaphor. It could be taken literally, as if God were an extra organ alongside your heart and lungs. Or a part of your mind, like your memory. The problem is that we can't find God the way we can scan for a heart, and God doesn't become part of us the way our memories are. It's more like we make space for God – by listening, by opening ourselves, by getting together with other people who also want God's presence – and when that works, we are able to embody God or do what God wants rather than what we want.

That of God. If, in the common Quaker phrase, we have 'that of God within', what is 'that of God'? A piece of God? No, surely God can't be cut up into bits like a cake. A portal to God, like a telephone? A drop of God-ish-ness, like a little bit of salt in fresh water? A capacity to God, an ability to do God things, a power to enact God, a potential to act Godishly in the world? I think this last option is getting closer, but it's often unclear.

'Within', inside, inwardness, are directional metaphors like the 'height' and 'depth' metaphors uncovered by Anglican writer John Robinson in his 1963 book *Honest to God*. God has, he argues there, often been pictured 'up', in 'the heavens' – sometimes literally, with clouds or in the sky. This image can be inspiring and it works with some aspects of the human body (physically looking up can lift our mood), and it goes with the sun as the source of light on earth and other aspects of our metaphorical system ('up' is usually 'good' or 'bigger' – the stock market is abstract and doesn't have to 'rise' and 'fall', but it does, and those terms embed a value; see George Lakoff and Mark Johnson's book *Metaphors We Live By*, new edition 2003, for more about this). On the other hand, as Robinson says, it also fails badly for many modern people, who live after the age of rocket launches and know that moon landings are possible. Today, it's hard to imagine 'heights' as God's domain. Instead, Robinson suggests we seek God in the depths – within ourselves and the world, by going down the roots instead of up to the mountain-tops. This is equally metaphorical but having more and richer metaphors can help to express a complex truth.

Godding. In English a lot of possibilities become nouns, assumed to be concrete, in the absence of other evidence. Even our generic words, like 'thing', are for nouns. The word 'God' is a noun. But God might not really be a thing; it might be more useful to think of God as an action, a verb. (David Cooper wrote a good book about this view from a Jewish perspective, called *God Is a Verb* – Berkley, 1998.) In the book I use the word 'God' in the familiar grammatical pattern, as a noun, because writing sentences in plain English where someone was inwardly godding rather than sensing God within became confusing and unreadable. But the God I am talking about is not necessarily concrete in any familiar sense. Some nouns are for things we expect to be able to track down and count: one chair, two tables, a book, some socks, no sheep. Other nouns are more abstract: sense, love, experience, time, calm. Many English nouns can also serve as verbs anyway – a love, my love, loving; a calm, to be calm, calming – and I think that keeping this possibility in mind will help get at the nature of God more accurately.

Lord. There are a lot of common words for God which I don't use in this book. In some cases that's because I have a specific objection to them or because I know they create particular problems. For example, although I think that God is a being of all genders and none, I don't use any gendered terms for God in this book. I don't call God he, she, they, or it; I repeat the word 'God' even when a pronoun would be usual in English. I have also chosen to avoid words which suggest that God might be in a hierarchy, with power over us. Although calling God 'Lord' can be a powerful political statement – the speaker takes God as lord and ruler, not any earthly government – this isn't always understood and the gendered and political associations of words like 'Lord' get in the way sometimes. It's more important to me, in this book, that I am able to describe God as within and alongside us, and all the material world, than to make that specific point. (I think that people who are convinced by what I propose here, that we can see the guidance the inner voice gives and benefit from it, both individually and as a community, will get to the need to value that guidance over constructs like nations and political parties anyway.)

Jesus Christ. Ah, Jesus, old friend, what are we to do about you? Jesus can be seen as the embodiment of the Light. Jesus can be seen as a great teacher. Jesus can be regarded as the son of God, or even God the Son. Jesus can be a problem, tying us to historical narratives and impossible claims and to views about other religions which range from the complex to the genocidal, with plenty of well-meaning and insulting options along the way. Jesus, overall, is often ignored by modern liberal Quakers. From a mixture of ignorance, discomfort, anxiety, a sense of irrelevance, and other difficult feelings, it can be hard to pick out what liberal Quakers find good about Jesus. It is there – Jesus as role model, Jesus as teacher, the mystic Christ within – but as a weaker theme than at some points in Quaker history. Having plenty else to grapple with in this short book, for the time being I leave Jesus mainly to his own devices. (I hear he can overcome some pretty dire challenges.) I won't be discussing Jesus Christ explicitly – but if you think you've spotted his influence somewhere in these pages, you are probably right. Let's call that an Easter egg.

Spirit. Some Christian theologies, with an emphasis on the Trinity, talk about the Holy Spirit one of the three Persons within the one God. Quakers, who have this idea in the background, aren't very worried about the details of it, and having dropped the patriarchal image of God the Father and opted to mainly ignore the Son are left with a general idea of God as Spirit. The idea of spirit, immaterial or maybe like air or breath, moving and present with us, can be a powerful one. In today's world, the relationship of the word 'Spirit' to 'spiritual' may be helpful. Lots of people are 'spiritual but not religious', sensing some depth to their experience but not wanting to engage with formal and structured faith, and the idea of the movement of the Spirit may speak to that freedom. Although Quakers have structures, we don't have many of the things people associate with formal religions – we have leaders, but we take turns in those roles; we have theology, but we hope you come to agree with us by testing rather than because someone tells you to; we have traditions, but we can explain why we do things and are willing to change when appropriate – so there is room in our community for this kind of freedom, too. Like the wind blowing, the Spirit moves invisibly; the Quaker community feels for that movement and tries to follow, like a kite. We may not succeed but we can often head in the right direction.

Divine. I talk about the divine sometimes in the hope that this more abstract word has fewer of the difficult associations of some of the terms already mentioned, and also for a change. Like 'Spirit', 'divine' helps to get away from the image of God as a physical being. It can also be used as an adjective to describe a noun: 'divine something', as in 'divine Presence', and in that way helps to clarify sentences. I hope it's clear throughout that although I think we can know some things about what the divine is like because of the experience we have with it, there's also a lot we don't know.

Capitalised Words. Some Quaker writers – Jim Pym is a good example – can capitalise almost any noun and bring to it the significance of holiness. This is a good way of extending lists of possible words for God: Light, Spirit, Love, Universe, Energy, Presence, Flame, Water, Bread, Beloved... In this book, I try and avoid the temptation to coin too many of these, trying to stick to the plain word God and a few others which help the reader to understand what I'm talking about. Once in a while, though, another aspect needs a new word and I will sometimes use this technique.

Language is tricky. It is human and full of omissions and errors. But I think human language, with patience and work, can be as good as any other human thing – as good as any other human way of knowing, for example. That being so, although I don't expect to get to the top of the mountain, I see no reason not to set out and climb towards a perfect expression of the incomprehensible God that I glimpse in the distance.

How We Know – Listening Together

At the beginning of this book, I made some big claims about what Quakers know. What is the basis of those claims? What kind of evidence can we offer for the things we think we know, and how do Quakers come together to know as a community things which our surrounding society might think of as personal and private beliefs?

When people try to offer evidence in the area of religion, there are lots of options – all of them open to question, as any atheist or student of philosophy of religion will know. Traditional arguments often centre on the question of whether or not God exists. For example, someone might point to the beauty of the world as evidence and say that this suggests that God exists. That might be the case. It can certainly be an enjoyable process for believers to engage in: looking at flowers, sunsets, babies, and apple pie, and praising God for God's goodness. The problem is that not everything in the world is beautiful, and deadly nightshade, earthquakes, genocide, and poverty all suggest that either God doesn't exist or doesn't love us that much after all. Here we are into another traditional set of arguments, often called the problem of pain or the problem of evil. Responses on the believer's side can include suggesting that these things are somehow good from another perspective – everything is beautiful in God's eyes, even if humans can't see it, perhaps; or experience of bad things gives us an opportunity to develop into better people, improving our souls even while we suffer.

Plenty of textbooks have dealt with these debates and I'm not intending to repeat them all here. It is important, though, for me to acknowledge both their existence and their inconclusiveness. Some Quakers will accept traditional arguments based on observations like the way the world is suited for us to live in, from the need for a first cause, or similar. Others would reject them, and many would try to balance religious and scientific explanations: evolution and the Big Bang can have happened in a world where the God we experience is also real. Arguments of this form, where the evidence is based on observations about the world and trying to construct a logical chain linking the world to God, may be relevant to the prayer or belief of individual Quakers, but they are not of the same structure as the Quaker case I want to put forward here.

Before I get to the Quakers, I want to consider another source of evidence which might be included as evidence for God and what God is like. In many traditions, a scripture or tradition – something handed down from previous generations – tells people about God. For example, the Methodists say that there are four sources: scripture, tradition, reason, and experience. The scripture in this case is the Bible, a complex set of books which record the spiritual (and other) experiences of Jewish and Christian people over a long period of time. Many Quakers would include the Bible, and other spiritual writings, as giving us some evidence about God. But unlike the Bible, which is closed and cannot be added to or changed, it is possible to have a tradition which is open and growing. Many religious groups do this in different ways. The Quakers are explicit about it – about the idea of continuing or progressive revelation and the need to update things regularly.

The basis for this updating is religious experience. This was included as the fourth of the Methodists' four ways of knowing about God, and is part of many traditions. The Quakers take it especially seriously, and as I will soon show, they have put some safeguards in place against the ways in which it might go wrong as a source of information. In particular, where other groups test new ideas against the experiences of previous generations and especially the Bible, meaning that they can only change fairly slowly, Quakers sometimes test new revelation among the group, aware of previous experience but not taking it as a final authority, meaning that they can sometimes change relatively fast.

Hold on, you might reasonably say at this point. Religious experience isn't evidence of anything. For one thing, it might just mean that someone is hallucinating. Having a vision or hearing voices doesn't prove that you had direct contact with God. Our brains are tricky things and we can easily be misled by what seem to be convincing experiences. And besides, there are plenty of cases of people who had religious experiences in which God told them to do something horrible. Both of those things are true – although Susan L. DeHoff has argued (convincingly in my opinion) in a 2018 book called *Psychosis or Mystical Religious Experience?*, that people like pastors and mental health professionals who listen to lots of such accounts are usually able to distinguish the two. One of the key tests is their fruit – does the experience tend to make the person and those around them happier and healthier, or not? As well as working out the difference on an individual basis, Quakers try to address these problems by working together in communities to test the guidance they are getting from God.

I'll come back to the point about the importance of the community, but before I do, I need to address another possible issue – what if this idea that experience gives us knowledge falls down at the first hurdle, when we try and move from a completely private experience to expressing it in language.

Some people have argued that it doesn't make sense to try and think of 'experience' as something which exists outside language. I'm going to use the work of Anglican nonrealist theologian Don Cupitt as an example here because he is clear, focused on religious questions, widely read and discussed by Quakers who adopt nonrealist (including fictionalist and nontheist) views about God, and slightly wrong but in interesting ways.

Cupitt says that instead experience, such as there is, is formless and entirely individual. People can't compare experiences, he argues, without translating them into language – and so there's never any real, distinct thing called 'experience' which can be brought into language to validate it. People can't, he thinks, check impressions of something by comparing with someone else's impressions – because it's never really a process of comparing impressions, only whether the people trying to compare impressions have learned to use the same words. Instead, everything is language. In his book *What Is a Story?* Cupitt makes a strong case that not only can stories serve lots of purposes, they are everything humanity has got. People live within in stories – today, not usually within a single narrative but with lots of competing stories being told and retold all the time – and as human beings every one of us lives within language. For Cupitt, this is a good thing. It frees people from metaphysical mistakes that might have been made in the past, like trying to pin down God's existence in the material world. It gives space for people to choose their stories and retell them in ways which work for the tellers and their current situations.

This view might be thought to present a very big problem for the argument I am making here. If there is only language, how can I make these claims that Quakers know anything about the real world? Hasn't Cupitt just shown that we can't use the kind of comparative methods I describe Quakers using?

I don't agree. I think there are two mistakes here: a mistake in Cupitt's own work, where language is both nothing and everything at once; and a mistake in working out the implications for what I'm saying.

In Cupitt's writing, he starts by elevating story, and with it language. We live in stories. Language forms our whole world. (Not the physical world – I don't think Cupitt denies the existence of the world or the fact of our experiences of it, only the reliability of the connection between sense impression and language, especially once we are into the less concrete matters of religion.) Language is, on this view, very important. Then he tries to minimise experience by reducing it to language – comparing our sense impressions is just language, it isn't really a check on anything. Trying to bring experience into language while maintaining its accuracy, to somehow keep it on both sides of the barrier – real-out-there and expressed-in-words – is incoherent, he says. But by his own argument, that language is important, this isn't really a reducing but a lifting up. 'Experience' might not function as a cross-check with the material world, as some want it to, but even if it is entirely within language it can function as a comparison between people. We know that we can agree or disagree on what happened or what something is like, and even if this is only taking place within the linguistic world, it can be used for the same functions within a community as it would if it did refer to a 'real world'. If everything is language, language matters – a lot! – within social groups, and so this comparison process remains just as important in a world where it's all about stories as it would be if the comparison crossed the boundary to the external world.

So that's a mistake within Cupitt's own work – in my opinion. You are welcome to form your own opinion about it, especially in light of my next point: that it doesn't affect my position very much. I'm sympathetic to some of Cupitt's points, especially about the importance of language, but I think he goes too far in some ways, especially in underestimating the extent to which people in the same place at the same time can have a shared experience. I also think, though, that in light of the mistake I just identified in Cupitt's argument, even if he is right about more of this than I think, that wouldn't prevent my argument from working.

Suppose I am wrong about shared experience and Cupitt is right – there's no such thing as shared experience at all. Even if you are sitting next to me and we are looking at a table together, we are not having the same experience. If that's the case, then what we compare when we try and compare experiences of the table is really whether we have learned to use the same words for the experiences we have in relation to the table. We can describe it: it's rectangular, it's this high, it's brown, it's handy for putting cups of tea on. We might disagree on other points: I think it's quite nice, you might find it ugly. Unless we are to go down a path of deep scepticism, in which we know nothing about the table for sure despite being able to agree on an important set of descriptions, we can still say that we know these things about the table. In Cupitt's picture, we only know these things within the world of language, being unable to use experience to reach outside that; but we still know them, so in practice, the argument I am making about Quaker knowledge will run in much the same way.

Hopefully that exploration has established that whether or not religious experience connects to an external deity, Quakers can use religious experience within our linguistic world as a way to know things. How do we go about being sure of what we think we know in this situation?

Quakers generally think it's safer if the group are all led, not by a person but by God, in the same direction. If that direction is also in line with the things Quakers have previously been led towards – peace, justice, truth-telling – the leading is being tested by the present and past community. This isn't perfect. Quaker groups have made mistakes and thought that they were led towards things which we can now consider to be wrong, and probably we are still making mistakes. The Quaker meetings who held out in favour of enslavement, for example: even when some Quakers were calling for an end to slave owning, some Quakers – often those who were holding people in slavery – tried to find Quaker ways of supporting that evil system. There can also be disagreement. Two Quaker meetings facing the same question might arrive at different answers – at the moment, for example, there is disagreement among Quakers internationally, and sometimes within the same Quaker community, about equal marriage. When a community reached a clear conclusion, it often took a long time – for example, Quakers in Britain decided in 2009 to start conducting same-sex weddings, but that decision came after a process lasting at least twenty years.

No system of testing which relies on human input will be perfect. Even mechanised and computerised systems are open to developing errors – or inheriting them from their human inventors. However, the Quakers working as a group are better off than an individual relying on their personal religious experience, because they can draw on more evidence. And they are better off than a community which relies only on a written text or unchanging rules, because they can bring in new evidence and respond to changing conditions. In some areas, Quakers have had a notably consistent message over long periods of time, and sometimes a sense of strong guidance in one direction can unite and energise a community like very little else.

So far, this section has been entirely theoretical. How do Quakers actually go about sharing religious experience? Is that even possible? And what kinds of answers do Quakers arrive at which might suggest that they are getting messages from something other than themselves, rather than just reaching a consensus?

Stay with me for just one more theoretical point, then I'll get to the practical. The last theoretical point is about religious experience. When I use that phrase, I find that people often assume I mean a private, mystical experience: a vision of the divine, an overwhelming sense of connectedness or joy, a voice which speaks directly to you... all of these and many more are important forms of religious experience. These are included among the 'mystical religious experiences' which DeHoff asked about when she looked at whether it's possible to distinguish these from hallucinations.

However, the word 'experience' covers a lot of other things as well. Think about experiences you might give as a present: a trip to the cinema or the zoo, a skydive or a stargazing trip. You can share those experiences. You might be unable to share the *exact* experience that your loved one has – if I watch a sunset with my sibling who has some colourblindness, we probably don't see the same thing – but you have experienced it together. (It would sound silly to say that we'd seen two different sunsets.) Going on a Christian pilgrimage, attending a Buddhist meditation session, or going to Quaker meeting for worship together is a shared experience in this sense. These are also examples of religious experiences.

Together, then, the Quakers aim to share our experience of listening to the Light Within. By doing that we expect to be able to weed out mixed messages – to make sure that we are hearing God and not our own opinions or the demands of the world around us – and to be strengthened, as a community, to act on what we're told.

I realise that this has been a short summary and you might still have questions. Please come on social media and ask me! However, in order to keep this book a Quaker Quick, rather than a Quaker Tome, I'm going to hope that you have seen enough of the logic and structure of the Quaker argument to go along with it for now, even if you can't agree with it at every step. What does this theory look like in practice?

At the core of the practice is the listening. Waiting in silence, Quakers try to set aside daily concerns and bring everything into the Light, asking God to help us see and hear the truth. Let me help you to imagine this by describing some real meetings where people do this. Many Quakers meet for unprogrammed worship once a week – often but not always on a Sunday morning, typically for an hour but maybe for thirty minutes or two hours, sometimes in a purpose-built meeting house, sometimes in a private home or via videoconferencing. Most people who belong to a group who worship in this way are also invited to attend a meeting for worship for business, in which the unprogrammed method is, perhaps paradoxically, combined with an agenda to provide an opportunity for the community to try and hear any guidance on the decisions they need to make.

The meeting for worship for business can be held at any mutually convenient place and time (including online or by phone). The method can be used with a small group of people or a big group; I've attending meetings for worship for business with anywhere between four and a thousand people. One difference between the different sizes of meeting is how strict you need to be in order to make it work smoothly. The more people there are, the more restraint each person needs to show, and the worse things can go wrong if someone doesn't stick to the discipline required. Some of that discipline will be practical – if the group have chosen to use microphones to improve accessibility, for example, then everyone who wants to speak needs to wait to be given the microphone. Other parts of the discipline are spiritual – because we believe that our Quaker method can help to work out, not just what we want, but what God wants, everyone who is going to speak should make sure that they really feel they are being led to speak, and not just sharing their own ideas or desires.

A similar method can be used for lots of types of decisions. Meeting for worship for business is typically used for points which concern the whole community – for agreeing how to spend money owned by the community, for admitting people to membership and appointing them to roles within the community, for working out how the community will react to issues in the wider world, and so on. The purpose of this method is to help us to look for God's voice and listen to the Light. When we tune in correctly, we can get insights into situations and possibilities which wouldn't usually occur to a group using another method – taking a leap beyond compromise into radical answers. We can approach complex questions with a level of compassion and tenderness to all involved which is difficult to hold without the space created by this method. We can apply this method to all sorts of questions: to asking how we can and should communicate with God, to asking how we should respond to a global crisis, to thinking about how to explain our experiences to others. Whatever the question, in meeting for worship for business, we try and look with God's eyes. Through them, we can access another dimension of humanity.

That might sound weird. It *is* outside the current culturally normal ways of doing things, although I don't think it's supernatural – rather, it's a way of getting to what is most natural and sensing how to work with the flow of the world. It is also intensely powerful and many people who have experienced it working well, including me, become inclined to say dramatic things about it, like, 'this is how we know what the Light is saying to us'.

How We Know – Recording What We See

In the previous section, I described the way in which a Quaker meeting for worship for business works. It's based on the process Quakers use in all meetings for worship, of using silence as a tool to listen for what God, or the Light, or the Spirit, or the Christ Within, is telling us. I left out a step, though. In meeting for worship for business, we need to make a record of what we have heard. There are various ways of doing this, but the most theologically interesting – and perhaps the most difficult in practical terms! – is simultaneous minuting. In simultaneous minuting, the people in the meeting write down and agree a statement about what they have heard during the meeting itself. It's most practical to appoint someone, a clerk, to do the actual writing, although sometimes someone else in the meeting can offer exact wording to the clerk. The minute usually only records the facts and the decision. In other systems, minutes are often taken as notes and written up later to be agreed at the next meeting. This isn't needed with simultaneous minuting, because although someone might produce a neat copy later, the real text of the minute has been agreed in the meeting itself. This also means that the minutes do not record everything which was said. Instead, they aim to capture the most essential points.

In meeting for worship for business, Quakers aim to sense God's will for a specific group at a specific time. I'm going to spend time on the details of the process in this chapter because those details reveal some interesting things about the Quaker relationship with God. I begin with the process of writing the minutes, even though in the meeting itself this is often a later or final step, because it's in this step that the Quaker community demonstrates our commitment to identifying and recording a fact – discerned or sensed by those present – about what the Light is calling the group to do. I move on to look at some of the ways in which other aspects of our understanding of the Divine, such as the equality of all, are modelled in this process, and some of the ways in which it can go wrong.

The work of sensing when the group has reached unity, and reflecting that in the minute, a document written in the presence of and in cooperation with the group, requires confidence and skill on the part of the clerks, usually in a team of two or three. It also needs a good deal of support and patience from the group. The process of offering silent support while the work is done is called 'upholding' and also brings us back to the spiritual basis on the Quaker decision-making method. The Light within each person calls out to the Light within the others, forming a community which is connected and loving.

When this works well, it can even hold through a conflict. I don't want to make exaggerated claims here, or suggest that this is unique to the Quaker community – Quakers are as capable of falling out as anyone else, and lots of people are able to hold together an underlying friendship even while they disagree about something significant. However, I think it's important to describe some of the ways in which this happens to work among Quakers, because it helps to illuminate some of the principles which underlie the process. One is that our time is not the same as God's time. Just because a decision seems urgent doesn't mean that it can be rushed. Quaker meetings which are struggling or unclear about an answer often need to delay it until another time. (In fact, research by Nicholas Burton and others into the Quaker business method reveals that it's probably slower than other methods for simple decisions, and faster than other methods for complex decisions.)

One of the principles which Quakers identify in our method is that everyone is equal. This doesn't mean that everyone is assumed to know the same things – obviously they don't – or that everyone is expected to think the same way – we wouldn't get far if we tried to make that happen – but that everyone's voice is given equal value. Everyone is trying to listen to find the way forward, and everyone has equal access to the Light within. That means that anyone in the room, even someone who might be thought not to understand the question or who is out of step with the rest of the group, might be led to the answer. In small groups, we usually try and hear everyone who feels moved to speak. In larger groups where this is sometimes impossible, clerks try to sense who needs to be heard, rather than wondering who is likely to give the answer they want to hear! Sometimes a clerk will call on someone with specific knowledge to answer a factual question, but once the facts have been established, weighing different factors and suggesting possible answers falls to everyone.

However, this is a process used by humans, and although we try and get closer to God, we can always make mistakes. A common mistake is to give more weight to one person's opinion because of their previous experience or role in the community. Now, on the one hand, it might seem obviously sensible to trust someone who works as an accountant when you're making a financial decision, for example, or to weigh the opinion of someone who's been in the community a long time over that of a newcomer. There are simple decisions where you might decide to do that – perhaps not even using the Quaker business method with a large group to decide which bank to use for a new account, for example, but handing that over to a committee. But there are also decisions which go deeper: even something which is apparently about money might also be about ethics, about risk taking, about priorities and prior commitments. In those cases, someone who is used to making these decisions using the logic of the dominant culture (thinking, for example, about the rate of return on an investment as the most important thing) might struggle to switch over to trying to find the way forward which God wants for the community (should we focus on investing in something which is socially useful even though it doesn't make as much money? or in this case does God want us to make sure that the community has an income into the future, and think about the returns on our investment as well?). Balancing the roles of expertise and experience with open-mindedness and inspiration is a challenge in any decision-making process. The Quaker way aims to be flexible enough to allow this balance to shift depending on the nature of the decision which the meeting is considering.

Another mistake is to misjudge the nature of the decision. Some decisions are best left to a professional or a small group who become expert. Others need to involve the whole community, but people aren't able to go straight to decision-making – for example, if a question is highly emotive, people might need space to share those feelings and be heard before they can go into a meeting for worship for business to make a decision. Participating in the process needs us to be present, which usually requires feeling our feelings, but also open, able to respond to the feelings of others, and to sort out where stuff is coming from. I might want the meeting to decide to keep everything just as it is because that makes me feel safe. That's fine and might need to be shared – but it also might not be the whole story. Someone else wants the meeting to change the layout of the building because that would make it easier for them to access it. How can I sit with my need for security and their need for access, and work out what we are being led to do?

If we take a vote or a leader decides, there are winners and losers. In the Quaker meeting for worship for business, it is often possible to bring everyone along together, even if some of them are supporting the unity of the meeting rather than the decision itself: uncertain or not in agreement, but seeing the need to reach and stand by an answer. Of course, even that isn't always possible: sometimes we have a strong leading and go for it even though a few people in the community can't see why or struggle to accept the decision. Sometimes we need to go ahead and let there be a time for grief and adjustment. In other matters, it's possible to go slowly and find ways forward which will be seen as following God's guidance in future, even if they are hard to take at the time. This is easiest to see looking further back. Quakers now celebrate our role in the anti-slavery movement, even though some Quaker pioneers in this area were accompanied by many Quakers who struggled to give up the practice of enslaving people, kept treating people as property despite seeing that it was wrong, and didn't necessarily move faster than their surrounding culture. (You can read all the details of this story in Donna McDaniel and Vanessa Julye's 2009 book *Fit for Freedom, Not for Friendship*.) Meeting for worship for business does not make things easy or make it possible for us to be anything other than the flawed human beings we are. It does ask us to chill out – 'Be still and cool in thine own mind and spirit' as George Fox famously put it – so that we can listen and look for the guidance God is offering.

Some of that guidance is just for a particular time or place. The renovations to a meeting house don't need recording for other Quakers to hear too. Other guidance is for sharing. Meetings might exchange minutes or letters, called epistles, as well as visiting each other and forming personal connections between members. Over the years, bodies of useful texts have been built up. Starting out as hand-copied collections of minutes written by Yearly Meetings (basically AGMs for groups of Quaker meetings), the tradition of collecting helpful stuff has built up into a whole range of books. Some are called books of discipline, others books of faith and practice, and all aim to bring together guidance received in meeting for worship, decisions we might need to refer to, and material which might be helpful or inspiring to us as disciples, people on a path of following God's will. They vary a lot in their emphasis and particularly during the twentieth century there has been a shift from books which mainly speak in a corporate voice – we do this, we say that – to collections of quotations from individual writers – I do this, someone else says that. In general, though, they all collect stuff which can help to guide Quakers in practical and theological ways.

And what guidance do they actually offer? In the following sections, I'm going to dig deeper into some of the things Quakers have recorded, through materials collected in their books of faith and practice. By exploring some books of faith and practice in detail, I hope to show something of what Quakers know about God and how they act on that knowledge.

What God's Voice Showed Central and Southern Africa

In the slim book *Living Adventurously* (also available online), the Quakers of Central and Southern Africa Yearly Meeting have tried to record what they know about God. They say that they aim to 'capture our experience, concerns, witness and insight from living our faith' in the specific context of central and southern Africa. In putting together this book, they have tried to collect the writings of Quakers, and something of their oral tradition, to build up a picture of what they have heard by listening to God. This includes material which is unique to the context – using the African concept of Ubuntu or dealing with South Africa's history with apartheid, for example – but also experiences of meeting for worship which would be recognised by Quakers around the world.

In this section, I want to explore in detail some of the passages from *Living Adventurously* which reveal most about what these Quakers know about God. When Quakers collect insights into a book like this, there is still a diversity of understandings, but what is presented has been tested. It may have been initially written by an individual or a small group; it has been read and selected by a committee who discerned its usefulness; and it has been approved by a Yearly Meeting who will be referring to it for many years to come. A Quaker book of faith and practice is never the final answer, but it does contain answers.

So what do the Quakers of Central and Southern Africa know about God? To start with, here's a passage from their chapter on 'Our experiences of meeting for worship':

A Ministry which is the revelation of God communicates to the members of the meeting. When there is oneness in the spirit of the worship, when the Spirit reveals itself, each and every one of the worshippers experiences its presence as it communicates with each and every one of us. (Kholekile Tshanga, Cape Eastern Monthly Meeting, South Africa, *Southern Africa Quaker News*, September, 1999)

In this passage, Tshanga talks about the direct connection between God and the worshippers which I have been discussing. (The 'Ministry' referred to in this context is probably a spoken ministry, a message someone in the meeting is led to deliver into silence.) In this passage, the connection is identified as one which enables communications – Tshanga doesn't use the metaphors of hearing or seeing, talking instead about experiencing presence. He also makes it clear that this is not an automatic experience. There could be a problem with the group who are worshipping, who can't reach oneness for some reason. But when it works, it includes everyone who is present. The God who is revealed here, in Spirit, is one who is present, who communicates, and who speaks not just to a few people, but to the whole community.

This is reflected in another passage – here, notice how the emphasis is on connection with the divine but the community is implied by the use of the plural pronoun, 'we'.

Quaker worship is spiritual not sacramental. It is mystical worship – direct connection with the Source. We do not deny the material world, but we look to the spiritual dimension and constant heart to heart contact with the Source, in order to bear Fruit. (Jennifer Kinghorn, South Africa, 'Mystery, Mysticism and Daily Living: A Quaker Adventure', Richard Gush Lecture 2005, *Living Adventurously*, p. 32)

The connection is individual, through the heart, but it is also collective. Some Quakers would flip the claim about sacramentality – we can also say that all life is sacramental – but the point is clear: it is not through a particular sign or moment that God reaches us. Instead, we can access the Source within ourselves. Kinghorn signals the way some words are being used to refer to the divine with capital letters. Source is one of these, but she also mentions Fruit. This leads into the way in which Quakers bring back something from their connection to the spiritual dimension, bringing it into the material and social world in the form of action.

This is also reflected in Ros Posemann's description, page 11, of finding in meeting for worship: 'An immediate sense of being still in the presence of God.' Presence, stillness, and immediacy are familiar ideas by now. There are also quotations which suggest the diversity of people's experience and respect for their individuality. Zimbili Mabazo, for example, says (page 15) that in silent meeting for worship 'you could connect with God in your own way.' In this comment, Mabazo expresses both the directness of the connection people feel in meeting for worship, and the flexibility to connect 'in your own way'.

The connection described may not happen, or not consciously, for everyone or every time, but the words which are picked out to be included in the community's book – words which speak to lots of people and where the experience is recognised by lots of people – describe this experience. This is not a distant God, but a present one. This is not a God who wants you to be or pretend to be something you are not, but a God you can connect with in your own way. This is a not a God who requires something special before getting in touch. This is a God who is there and listening right now. In return, we listen to God.

Another quote in *Living Adventurously*, from Mary A. Holmes on page 27, talks about this relationship between God and people. 'God, or spirituality, is in every human being. The divinity is called "the Light". The Light is in everyone, although it burns more brightly in some than in others.' Again, this quote describes God as right here and right now. God is within every human being. The Light of God in everyone might be hidden or not able to burn brightly for some reason – and this explains why we don't all sense it or sometimes meet someone and can't see anything of God in them – but it is there. The process of listening to the Light Within and acting under the guidance it provides is a way of making it burn brighter or show more clearly. We can connect this with the previous quotes, and added together, they give an account of how Quakers experience God. In stillness, Quakers are aware of God's presence. They connect with God directly, in their own ways and not by doing what someone else tells them to. They know that this connection is open to everyone who wants it.

They also know that through this connection, they are guided to act in certain ways. Quakers have a faith which is not just theoretical but in which there is a Light that guides people to act in loving ways. In *Living Adventurously,* Quakers have collected examples of this which are specific to the social and historical context of Southern and Central Africa as well as material which speaks to wider concerns. Here are two examples where the link between the religious motivation for the action and the action itself are especially clear.

The first is a passage from a letter sent in 1972, from Southern Africa Yearly Meeting to the South African Ethnic Auxiliary Committee, refusing to participate in apartheid (page 87):

The Religious Society of Friends in South Africa is a Christian community whose faith allows only one undivided membership. Consequently it is not possible for us to build into the Constitution of one of our subordinate bodies any distinction or separation of its members whether on an ethnic or any other basis.

(Quakers often call themselves Friends especially in the names of organisations and when speaking to other Quakers – this can be confusing, so I only use the word 'Quaker' in this book, but you will see the term 'Friends' used in some quotations.)

The second example is a quotation from Geoff Harris, who gave the Richard Gush lecture in 2003 on the topic *Is Peace Possible?* He said (pp. 85–6):

> We need to spread the news that the military has reached its use-by date. This follows from a belief that God never uses war to accomplish his/her purposes; from the fact that non-violent methods are less costly, more effective and able to be learned; from the fact that invasions have become rare, and that security needs [to] embrace far more than simply territorial security; and from the recognition that there are alternative ways of achieving security and cost effective non-military alternatives for the non-core functions which the military currently performs....

In these examples, and many others like them, Quakers draw a direct connection between the guidance we receive from the Light and the actions we take in the world. In Quaker thought, the two cannot be separated. We can join with others who are taking the same actions for different reasons, as Quakers often do in peace campaigning and other projects. The forms the actions take can vary a lot, and some of our community are drawn mainly to the work of prayer and maintaining awareness of divine presence. Still, through our listening in meeting for worship and meeting for worship for business, God's voice guides us as a community to both withdrawal – stillness, worship, and listening – and going out into the world – speaking truth to power and putting love into action.

What God's Voice Showed Britain

Many of the themes from Central and Southern Africa's book also appear in the books produced by Britain Yearly Meeting. Rather than repeat them in detail, I'll offer some examples which show the similarities between the two before going on to explore a development process which is especially obvious in Britain Yearly Meeting's books of discipline.

In Britain Yearly Meeting's current book, *Quaker faith & practice*, which was approved in 1994, there are lots of types of material. (I say 'current book' because a revision committee already exists to work on the next one – I'm on that committee – but the process has only just started, in 2019.) One way in which Quakers often cut them up is to think about the inspirational material on one hand – usually extracts from minutes or letters from meetings or writing from individuals, which helps to nourish a Quaker life – and organisational material on the other hand – typically guidelines for running Quaker communities and instructions from the Yearly Meeting on how to go about Quaker business. Britain Yearly Meeting's current book includes both, but historically and in many other Yearly Meetings this isn't the case. *Living Adventurously*, for example, doesn't go into procedural detail at all, while some books of discipline written in earlier times are almost all organisational. The inclusion of both in *Quaker faith & practice* gives an opportunity to look at passages which both explore the meeting for worship for business decision-making method described earlier in this book, and some which compare closely to the quotations from *Living Adventurously* explored in the previous section.

To give an overall feeling for *Quaker faith & practice*, here are some extracts which explore the themes I've already identified. What do Quakers know about God? We know that we can connect directly to the divine within us, that God is present in our lives and our meetings, that the Light can lead us and offer guidance, that we are inspired to take action because of our spiritual experiences, and that following our practices over a long period leads to growth and change in a person's life.

Here, for example, is Elizabeth Salisbury writing in 1968, in an extract from a longer passage (given as 2.58 in *Quaker faith & practice*):

[A]s the minutes ticked by and I sat in the healing peace [of meeting for worship], I began to be aware that something inside me was formulating a question which urgently needed to be asked. I say 'something inside me'; because it seemed at the same time to be both me and not me. I discovered to my horror that this something was urging me to get up and ask my question. My heart was pounding uncomfortably and I began to shiver....

Afterwards I found it difficult to believe that I had spoken. It was all over so quickly. Had I really stood up in front of all those people and testified? Well, hardly testified, but yes, I had been driven by some inner prompting which, for want of a more precise word, one might well call spirit; and yes, I had quaked, most fearfully, with something which was more than just the fear of making a fool of myself before family and friends.

The lack of a 'precise word' for an experience doesn't prevent Quakers from knowing. In this passage, Salisbury makes it perfectly clear that she experienced a kind of guidance which prompted her to speak and told her what to say. She isn't clear about whether it was internal or external to her – and while others might have opinions on this, we don't need to decide that question in order to affirm the reality of the experience and the significance of her contribution to the meeting for worship.

Like other Quaker works in what is broadly called the 'liberal' tradition, *Quaker faith & practice* owes a good deal to the ideas of Rufus Jones, one of the Quakers who in the early twentieth century worked to bring Quaker tradition and modern ideas together. Earlier in Chapter 2 than the Salisbury extract I quoted above, there's a passage from Rufus Jones which is very clear about the way in which unprogrammed or silent worship works as a tool for engaging with God's presence. It was written in 1937 and is given in *Quaker faith & practice* at 2.16 as follows – the square brackets were added by the committee compiling the book, not by me:

> [The early Friends] made the discovery that silence is one of the best preparations for communion [with God] and for the reception of inspiration and guidance. Silence itself, of course, has no magic. It may be just sheer emptiness, absence of words or noise or music. It may be an occasion for slumber, or it may be a dead form. But it may be an intensified pause, a vitalised hush, a creative quiet, an actual moment of mutual and reciprocal correspondence with God.

In this extract it's clear that Jones thinks of silence as a method or an action. The phrase 'a dead form' is related to the way in which early Quakers condemned the liturgy of the church as an empty form. They thought liturgy of repeated words, created by someone else, was lacking in life because it didn't relate directly to the individual's experience. Instead, a silence in which anything can be said is seen as not ritualistic because it's unplanned – but, by the time Jones wrote, Quakers had been using this practice of sitting in silence for hundreds of years. For some people, it can become just as much of an empty ritual, repeated without feeling, as any other form of worship. Having established that, though, Jones goes on to explore what happens in the silence when it's working well – intense feeling, life, creativity, and communication with the divine. That communication is, he says, 'mutual and reciprocal': it goes both ways.

To illustrate how this communication is direct and involves not just the individual, but the whole community, here's a short extract from early Quaker Francis Howgill, written in 1663 and given in *Quaker faith & practice* as 19.08, in a chapter with other historical writing.

> God out of his ever lasting love did appear unto us... when we had turned aside from hireling-shepherds' tents [from churches with paid ministers], we found him whom our souls loved.... The Lord of Heaven and earth we found to be near at hand, and, as we waited upon him in pure silence, our minds out of all things, his heavenly presence appeared in our assemblies, when there was no language, tongue nor speech from any creature. The Kingdom of Heaven did gather us and catch us all, as in a net.... We came to know a place to stand in and what to wait in; and the Lord appeared daily to us, to our astonishment, amazement, and great admiration....

Howgill describes not only his own experience, but something shared. He uses the plural first-person 'us' for the whole group – like I talk about 'we', the Quakers, in this book. The experience of God's 'heavenly presence' came when they were assembled together. It wasn't a one-off, either; Howgill says that it happened 'daily'. Modern Quakers include passages like this in their books because they recognise the experience. Some would describe it differently – very few would use the words 'Lord' or 'King' for God now, for reasons I'll discuss soon, and not all would say that something 'appeared', suggesting that it is outside us. But the core of the experience is familiar and people in meeting for worship can still feel the presence of God. We sometimes talk about a gathered meeting, one which is caught like Howgill's community in a net which pulls us towards God and the good.

My last extract from *Quaker faith & practice* is a short document which was approved by Britain Yearly Meeting (then called London Yearly Meeting) shortly after the First World War. Known as the Eight Foundations of a True Social Order, it tries to lay out a programme for building a better society – drawing on work Quakers were already doing but also looking to what else could be done. It is printed in full as passage 23.16 and I give four of the points here as a sample.

1. The Fatherhood of God, as revealed by Jesus Christ, should lead us toward a brotherhood which knows no restriction of race, sex or social class.

3. The opportunity of full development, physical, moral and spiritual, should be assured to every member of the community, man, woman and child. The development of man's full personality should not be hampered by unjust conditions nor crushed by economic pressure.

5. The spiritual force of righteousness, loving-kindness and trust is mighty because of the appeal it makes to the best in every man, and when applied to industrial relations achieves great things.

8. The ownership of material things, such as land and capital, should be so regulated as best to minister to the need and development of man.

The committee who were working on a draft of this book on behalf of Britain Yearly Meeting, though, didn't feel entirely comfortable with the language of this passage. They both recognised its importance as a major statement from the

Yearly Meeting, an authoritative gathering of the community, and the problems of the language which was used in it. To tackle this, they added a paragraph of preface before the Eight Foundations, which explains the historical context and ends with the observation:

> Though they proclaimed the ending of 'restrictions' of sex, they spoke of God as Father and human beings as men and brothers, as was conventional in their time.

Sometimes seeing through God's eyes means hearing the voices of people who are already within the Quaker community – but perhaps not being taken seriously. Britain Yearly Meeting, which includes England, Scotland, Wales, and the Channel Islands, has worked gradually and with mixed success to include more voices over a series of revisions to their book. The Yearly Meeting requested a new book in 1985, and the complete draft was brought back for approval in 1994, with the finished text agreed that year and published in 1995. Actually, it wasn't Britain Yearly Meeting which requested a new book – until 1994, this body was known as London Yearly Meeting. Someone who was there told me that it was seeing what this name would look like on the front of the book (previously it appeared inside) which prompted the change. It no longer felt acceptable to call the community only after a single city when the Quakers who belong to it live in a much wider area; although the annual sessions of Britain Yearly Meeting are often held in London, it can also meet in other places through the countries which it includes. Also reflecting this increased awareness of the geographical and political diversity of the Yearly Meeting community was the inclusion of Welsh-language passages.

Quaker faith & practice tries to reflect the reality of our current Quaker community in other ways, too. It changed some of the gendered language of previous versions, avoiding the use of generic 'he' for all people, for example, although as seen in the extracts above, the language was left in direct quotations. Quotations were chosen which reflected the concerns of the time – from sources ranging from the seventeenth to the twentieth century. The book also included passages from a wider variety of theological perspectives, and the second part of the book makes a clear effort to reflect disagreement and difference where it existed as well as unity around core Quaker themes.

This process tells us something about the way in which Quakers perceive God's guidance. The process took time and the community accepted that; listening to hear God's voice needs patience. Some parts of the book, especially the section called *Advices and Queries*, were tested with the whole community in draft form before being rewritten again for the final text. Other parts were added in response to comments on the draft, even during the Yearly Meetings which were held in 1994 to approve the text. A passage which used the term 'G-d/ess' was uncomfortable for many, and Jo Farrow wrote a companion passage which explains that, just as early Quakers used lots of new and experimental words for the divine, 'many women today are discovering a need to express their spirituality in ways which seem as strange to some Friends as the expressions of early Quaker spirituality did to those who first heard them' (passage 26.36, commenting on 26.35). The issues raised are similar to those I discussed in my chapter on language – naming and describing God, through all sorts of metaphors and comparisons, is a continual challenge.

In these two books, it's been possible to see the Quaker process at work and something of what God reveals to the Quaker communities involved. People have received guidance directly, by listening to the Light, and it's been tested by communities and found to be good. The guidance has encouraged those communities to move towards peace, social justice, and equality – even when that isn't easy and people take time to embrace it.

There have also been multiple perspectives and disagreements in both these books, about theology and ethics, and for my final example I want to look at Ireland Yearly Meeting, a book where it's more obvious in the text that the community have struggled to agree on what to include.

What God's Voice Showed Ireland

Ireland Yearly Meeting hasn't always agreed about what God was showing them. In producing their book of *Quaker Life and Practice*, Quakers in Ireland (the whole of the island of Ireland, that is – the Yearly Meeting covers both the Republic of Ireland and Northern Ireland) put a lot of effort in working out what they could say together. It wasn't easy. It also took a (fairly typical) eleven years: the revision work started in 1998, and the text was approved by Ireland Yearly Meeting in 2009 and published in 2012. On page 7, there's a description of the aims of the book and the problems which were involved in creating it:

> The book does not aim to be a complete statement of doctrine, nor to deal with all the obligations of discipleship, and still less is it to be regarded as a creed. Nevertheless, the wide spectrum of theological and cultural experience amongst Irish Quakers has come into focus during the preparation of this book and has resulted in much pain and difficulty.

Liberal Quakers wouldn't aim to produce a creed anyway, because being tied to a set form of words might prevent people within the community from expressing their faith as they experience it. As in other Yearly Meetings, Irish Quakers have a wide range of ideas about God and understandings of the divine. In particular, a distinction is often made between more Christocentric Quakers and more liberal Quakers. Christocentric Quakers, sometimes called Evangelicals (although that doesn't automatically mean they are similar to other churches called 'evangelical') focus on Christ, the Bible, and the relationship of Quakerism to other Christian churches. Liberal Quakers focus more on the direct relationship between God and the individual, and tend to see Quakerism as one faith among many rather than a specifically Christian church. There are significant points of agreement between them – all agree that the Quaker movement is historically part of Christianity, and that we can learn from God directly by listening, for example – but the difference of emphasis is enough that the two groups can be in conflict. They are even sometimes taken to be contradictory.

In the final version of their shared book, though, Ireland Yearly Meeting not only include passages which show what they all say and how they relate to the diversity of theology within their community. They also model, in the existence of the book itself and the process of creating it, something about what they think God is leading them to do. For one thing, they worked hard to make this happen – to work through and understand their disagreements and find a way to produce a book together despite that. The result is a book which shows this process in action as well as containing some distinctive material.

Comparing Ireland's book, *Quaker Life and Practice*, with Central and Southern Africa's book, *Living Adventurously*, and Britain's book, *Quaker faith & practice*, one of the things which stands out is the use of Biblical quotations. Although there are one or two in *Quaker faith & practice*, there are many more in *Quaker Life and Practice*. So far, I have only said a few vague things about the relationship of today's Quaker tradition to the Bible. In talking about possible sources of religious knowledge, I mentioned that some groups take the Bible as a source. (Some groups use other scriptures, but to keep this book a Quaker Quick I'm only going to talk about Quaker uses of the Bible here.) One way to think about liberal Quaker views of the Bible is to ask whether we view it as unique, as different but similar to other texts, or as one among many. Based on the Quaker understanding of direct communication with God which I've described so far, we might say that the Bible contains stories of, and sometimes direct reports from, people who also had that experience. In this perspective, it's one source among many because lots of other people, before and since, and in this and other cultures, have had the same experiences of directly connecting to the divine. However, some Quakers go further than that. In particular, the stories told by and about Jesus can be seen as explaining something about how the world works – especially how our relationship with God works – and as setting a pattern for our spiritual lives.

A wide range of views on the importance of Jesus are present in the Quaker community, and Quakers in Ireland may have a wider range, with more emphasis on scripture, and perhaps are more aware of the diversity, than the other two Yearly Meetings I've discussed in detail. The use of quotations from the Bible, more discussion of Jesus Christ, and a section on God the Creator – also rarely mentioned in the other two books discussed here – makes this visible in the text. As well as a wider internal diversity, Quakers in Ireland seem to be more aware of the need for their book to explain Quaker faith to other churches, perhaps because of their internal diversity and because of the broader social, political, and religious situation in Ireland.

Parts of a passage from Simon Lamb, section 1.104, help to explain this situation:

Ireland Yearly Meeting... has maintained strong and distinct Evangelical and Liberal wings under its care. These different traditions have sometimes struggled to stay in unity with each other... [but there are] many individuals in our midst who truly cherish diversity. They have understood that uniformity is no blessing.... We all sometimes need a spiritual thorn in the side....

In this extract, Lamb offers a way to think about the existence of these differences of understanding which brings it into line with what I have been saying about God's guidance. If it is diversity, and not uniformity, which is a blessing, it is possible that when Quakers disagree, it's not that some of them are hearing God correctly and others are not, but that all are being shown different aspects of the Light. A panel in the British embroidery project, the Quaker Tapestry, shows an image of white light passing through a prism and becoming a rainbow as a metaphor for this possibility. This can extend to the ways in which Quakers are led to act. Some will be led to hold very strong stances against war, for example, while others will find themselves called to work which involves being alongside armed forces. Here are two passages from *Quaker Life and Practice* which I think illustrate a little of this complexity.

Both are from Chapter 5, 'God: A God of Peace'. The first is the beginning of section 5.2, and it is in the corporate voice of Ireland Yearly Meeting, speaking together:

> The peace testimony is one of our most significant witnesses to the world. Friends hold to this expression of radical Christianity, and our testimony for peace has grown and deepened over the centuries....

This passage establishes the practice of peace, based on faith and following the non-violent model of Jesus, as very important to Quakers. Like other commitments which arise from listening to the Light, it is both part of the Christian tradition and something which has developed over time.

The second example is from near the end of the chapter and it's from the personal experience of James G. Douglas, a politician. In 1937, he said (as quoted in section 5.65):

> At the time I was asked to allow my name to go forward as a candidate for election, the country was in a state of civil war,

and membership of parliament involved the risk of loss of property and possibly even life. Under these circumstances I very clearly felt it my duty to stand for election, even though the State was defending itself by force against internal attack and the sittings of Parliament were guarded by military forces. I gave very little, if any, thought at the time to... the question of whether or not my position was or was not consistent with my membership of the Society of Friends. I did not seek public responsibility. When it came it seemed to be part and parcel of the work for goodwill which I believed to be the work God had given me....

In this explanation, Douglas displays a pattern I have discussed before – the sense of being given or led to specific work and taking that on, despite the challenges involved and the potential inconsistencies. The Quaker practice of accepting and valuing diversity doesn't just involve accepting the theological consequences of that – knowing that God is complex and the divine beyond human understanding – but also the practical consequences. The world is messy and doing good work in one way may mean accepting less than ideal situations; if Douglas had refused the help of the armed forces, he would probably have been unable to continue the political work which God had given him to do. To look for the leadings provided by God's voice does not mean avoiding risk – sometimes it means taking risk – and it doesn't mean getting things just right. It means moving forward in trust and doing the best we can with the opportunities and tools we have.

It also means having confidence, as Douglas does in this passage, that there is work which God gives us to do. It will be different depending on the time, the place, the person, and so on. It means knowing that guidance is available and hoping to have the strength to follow it. As Ireland Yearly Meeting put it in the postscript to *Quaker Life and Practice* (p. 220):

We pray to become a community where the power of the Holy Spirit is experienced enabling us to do what is right and freeing us from doing what we know to be wrong.

Is There Enough Evidence?

Where does all this leave us? In some ways, it leaves the Quaker community exactly where we started – we knew these things about the divine and ourselves all along, at some level. Perhaps we have now articulated them more clearly. Perhaps we can have more confidence in our conclusions having assessed the weight of the evidence which supports them. Perhaps having thought about the methods through which we gather and record that evidence, we can be more aware of the ways in which it helps us – especially to test and update what we know – and where it might go wrong.

What, if anything, does it do for readers who are not Quakers? Those of you who began with a religious belief of your own may have found points at which you can agree, and points at which you cannot agree, and some which are in between. Those who began with no belief might be able to see why I am convinced of my own position, or even agree that, if you had the same evidence to hand, you might agree with me. Others might be even more inclined to reject any sort of faith than you were before; you might consider me and the other Quakers delusional or misguided in a variety of ways, or have spotted something which is contradictory or hypocritical. Those who began with doubt might, just possibly, have been convinced by what I said.

In order to consider these issues in more detail, let me run through some of the points where I think various groups might agree or disagree. These are, of necessity, based on some generalisations about other communities – which opens up the possibility that members of those communities will disagree with me not just about the divine or about the evidence for God's direct communication with human beings, but also about how I have described their own communities. (People disagree within communities, too, in ways too complex to reflect accurately here.) Please regard my sketches as indicative of some possible positions. I hope to give enough of the reasoning in each case to enable you to adapt them to your own circumstances.

People of faith might agree about the experience of God communicating directly. This is not something exclusive to the Quaker community. Not all faith groups describe their experiences of divine communication in the same way, and not all use direct divine communication as part of their ongoing worship lives – but plenty do, and the sense of presence and guidance described in this book will be recognisable to many. This could be taken as supporting my position – more evidence that it does happen – but the existence of lots of different views about what God is and wants us to do complicate the picture. It could be argued that this only means direct communication with God is a common illusion, not a common reality. I think my arguments for the possibility of diversity within the Quaker community also apply to differences between religious traditions, but I also accept that it's a matter of degree – are they similar enough that this will stand? This will need to be assessed case by case, since religious traditions are too diverse to generalise about with confidence.

Alternatively, people of faith might disagree about the experience of God communicating directly. Even among those who accept the possibility, or that this happened in the past, not everyone considers this a trustworthy way of learning about God today. Even allowing for the Quaker method of testing communications within a larger group, communication from God in the present day with new content would be controversial in many religious communities. It could so easily be misguided or be from an evil source, either supernaturally or within the person. It would be better, someone who takes this view might reasonably think, to rely on established sources, such as tradition and scriptures. I don't find this convincing because those traditions and scriptures (usually) arose from people in the past having the same experience of direct communication – if it was possible then, why not now? If the message is different now, is that because it comes from a different source or because circumstances have changed and we now need to hear something new? I understand the worry about the source of the guidance, but when the new messages test well, producing good in the world, I reach the conclusion that it is the same God speaking to a new generation.

People whose world view does not include the divine might disagree about whether what I am describing is even possible. While accepting that some people have the experience of feeling connected to a 'divine', you do not have to accept that there is any such thing. Many people do not believe that there is a being external to humanity and/or the world which can be called 'God'. (I am, at least sometimes, one of them, so wait for the next twist.) The God I describe – which may have an unknown external aspect and may not, but is known through presence in the world and most easily identified within people, which may be thought of in a personal way but can also be imagined equally accurately as a form of feeling or energy – is a long way from traditional images of God and may not seem to deserve that name. Is it worth calling something 'God' if that God isn't necessarily all-powerful, for example? If you see that as a problem, consider whether or not it would be resolved by calling 'God' something else. Quakers, as I said earlier, also talk about the Light, Love, the Spirit, Energy, and many other names. For some this move is enough to solve the problem. If grasping a new understanding of the divine, and calling it by a name which moves away from previous images of what God is, doesn't help, fair enough. You may simply disagree on this point.

Another angle of objection is to ask what else I should accept, given that I have these beliefs, and to try to show that I should accept something ridiculous or contradictory. The mocking position which describes the divine as a 'sky fairy' or similar takes this approach. The God I describe in this book does not live in the sky or resemble a fairy in any significant way, unless fairies have recently taken up giving reliable guidance to carefully listening communities, so that example does not get far, but other arguments with the same structure work better.

For example, there is also a reduction to absurdity which involves taking the belief in direct guidance to individuals to a logical extreme. What if God orders you to murder someone? What about groups who commit atrocities in God's name? People do sometimes commit horrific acts under the impression that they are acting in accordance with God's wishes. In its simplest form, this objection ignores the communal testing which Quaker leadings undergo. However, the objection stands when that is taken into account, because even Quaker communities who try to test their leadings in the ways described here can cause psychological and emotional injuries and disagree with other Quaker communities. How can that happen? Everyone involved is human and can make mistakes. God's guidance may not be given all at once, or might be specific to a time and place. Whether you accept this objection may depend on how you assess Quaker actions overall. Do Quakers, in our peace work, campaigning, moves towards social equality, and other actions as led by God, do enough good to support the argument that this has indeed been guided by something all-loving? I haven't space here to present a full range of evidence on this point, so I will leave it by saying that I think we do – but then, I would say that. Quakers also make mistakes and it would be possible to construct a case full of historical examples to show that we have sometimes done harm or failed to do enough good. We may not be doing any better than other communities, and if you are considering joining the Quakers you will need to judge that for yourself.

An even stronger version of this objection might ask about

other experiences which have a similar level of evidence, such as bereaved people who are visited by their deceased loved ones. What should we accept on the basis of that? Some Quakers think that we should accept that this is evidence for people surviving after death in a non-physical form. (If you want to know more, look up the Quaker Fellowship for Afterlife Studies.) That might be right but I don't feel confident going that far. In the perspective of the objector, a belief in supernatural ghosts or a world of the dead parallel to the living world easily becomes ridiculous. How can that be avoided while taking the perspectives of both sides seriously? The experiences involved in the presence of a dead loved one are individual, rather than the collective experiences of being guided as a group which are part of the Quaker business method, so I don't think it's exactly comparable. I think the experiences of being visited which are reported by the bereaved are important and real, and we should be able to discuss and consider them – some have reported not being able to share these very moving experiences with their communities, which is sad. I tend to think of my own loved ones as dying and becoming (perhaps I should say remaining) part of the world: the physical body continues in the cycles of the natural world and the spiritual person continues in God. God was present within the person who died, and is within me, and so – just as the divine can form a loving connection between members of a community who are all together or meet through technology – God forms a connection between past and present, living and dead, in loving community.

You might find all this repulsive or unbelievable for some other reason. If you feel strongly about that, I'm impressed you got this far! I think it's important to acknowledge that some people have strong negative reactions to some or all religious ideas and talk – sometimes irrationally, sometimes rationally, sometimes for no apparent reason, sometimes from a specific past experience. Compare it to a negative reaction to seeing a snake: phobia, healthy respect, instinct, or having been bitten? These are all reasons to recoil from a snake. If you recoil from religion in the same way, okay. (I won't mind if you put this book down.) Sometimes, though, a negative reaction goes with a fascination and a desire to engage. I remember a circle dancing teacher telling the group that on her first encounter with circle dancing, she had hated it – holding hands reminded her of bad experiences at primary school, she didn't like being told how and when to move… but she also wanted to engage, to get closer to the thing which repulsed her, and find out why and understand it better. In the end she learned to love it and became a circle dancing teacher. Someone who responds to a snake that way might end up a zoo keeper. If you feel that way about religion – if you're repulsed but still reading, it might suggest that you do – perhaps you want to explore further.

There comes a point at which what I have described here cannot be described in any more detail or explored any further through writing. It has to be tested. In the next and final section of this book, I make some suggestions about how you could gather further evidence and evaluate it for yourself.

Testing the Core of Quakerism

How can the extraordinary claims made in this book be tested?

Some probably can't. Questions about whether the form of divinity described in this book as guiding and loving us should be called by the name 'God', for example, are not the sorts of things which can be settled by practical experiment because the answers rest in the social world. We simply have to pick a word and use it, and see whether our community will accept that pattern of use.

Other claims definitively can. Although 'experimentally' meant something more like the modern word 'experientially' in the seventeenth century when George Fox encouraged Quakers to 'know experimentally' the presence of God in each person, there are ways to experiment today with Quaker processes and see whether they hold up.

If you want to become an investigator, there are some simple experiments to try with this. You may wish to note down your results – spiritual journals, a genre in which past generations recorded their experiences, are well-established among Quakers.

The simplest experiment is to find a way to be quiet and listen. If you want to try this, it can be done alone or with a friend, indoors or outdoors, seated or lying down or walking, in bed at night or early in the morning or a few minutes during a lunch break, for two minutes or ten or thirty, in a physically quiet place or, paradoxically, in a place where surrounding noise or activity makes you aware of your own stillness. Settle yourself – Quakers call this centring down, and use images of coolness, calmness, stillness, and silence. Pay attention – be present and accept things as they are for the moment. Wait – you may sense a Presence or hear a Light. It may not be obvious or dramatic, but could be comforting, clarifying, or challenging. Noticing your own feelings and inner state can be part of the process. If something occurs to you, sit with it. You might like to imagine warmth, light, or another image of Love surrounding and supporting a person, situation, or process which is on your mind.

Many people find this is a good thing to do anyway. Some don't – trauma, mental health conditions, physical pain, and other issues can make it too difficult or distressing. If that's the case for you, other methods may work better for you: music, art, exercise, ritual, dance, counselling, dream analysis, focus objects, oracle cards, and probably many other things I've never thought about also help some people to focus and become aware of the Inner Light. Some Quakers use something like crochet or colouring to help them stay with the silence, even in meeting for worship. I'm not an expert on these and you would be well advised to consult other sources as well as doing your own experiments. For myself, if I use something other than silence I ask myself whether it's blocking or opening the parts of my self which God might use to reach me. I might be able to colour a picture in silence and still hear God, or listen to music in darkness and still see God. But if I'm colouring and listening to a podcast and smelling dinner cooking and... it's unlikely that I'll notice even if God's yelling! I'm a very verbal wordy person (you read my book, you know that!) so I find non-verbal activities like washing up and sewing to be most useful for settling myself. What works for you in the spiritual setting will depend a lot on your circumstances, personality, and history.

If you find the practice of being quiet and listening to be helpful, that's evidence as far as it goes that the Quakers are onto something in our methods. But because so many people find it helpful, without automatically having the same experiences with it or the same encounter with divine Presence, it doesn't go very far towards saying that the Quakers are right in the specific of our methods.

The crunch comes in working with others to test insights and leadings which arise in the silence. In this checking process we can produce stronger evidence. Multiple people are involved and have similar or overlapping experiences in as far as we are able to compare them. Guidance is found and the group finds a way forward – even where there may not be a single right answer, a best-for-now or good-enough answer can be identified. Sometimes the answers produced through the Quaker method are incredibly creative.

If you can find some friends who are up for it and identify a suitable question, you can try this for yourself. You might want to consult some of the resources listed at the end of this book for suggestions about the practicalities of this and the details of the theory. In general, it helps if you are clear about the question before the group, take time to listen, ask that people do not repeat points which have already been made, and appoint one or two people as 'clerks' to regulate the speed of contributions and write down a draft of the conclusion to be tested with everyone. So long as they are willing to cooperate with the practical guidelines, I find that it doesn't matter what the people present believe about the divine or direct guidance from God. Whatever God is or isn't, God – Love – the Inner Light – Spirit – the Ground of Being – can cope with some disbelief and doesn't abandon people for it.

Some researchers who were interested in this issue took the Quaker business method and tried using it with a secular business (Burton and Bainbridge published on this in the journal *Religions* in 2019). They found that the group were able to make decisions this way, without explicit reference to God or other religious terms. Although Quakers often regard the method as slow, the people in the company who used it said that it was quicker than other methods for complex decisions, probably because everyone's ideas got heard but without as much repetition. (It was slower for straightforward and minor questions, so the Quakers, who use it for almost everything, may be right as well.) Within a group using the Quaker business method, everyone is equal – the clerks have a special job but are there to serve the group, not boss it about – and so it was easier for managers to work with their teams. They found ways forward.

What sort of questions could you test with this? In a Quaker community, the questions we usually use to practice meeting for worship for business are those which affect the community specifically. We appoint people to take on tasks for a while, we agree patterns of meetings and discuss issues. We also talk about wider questions – especially if we can take an action. We might agree a boycott, support a protest, write a letter asking for a policy change, or ask everyone in our community to stop or start doing something as far as possible. As well as meetings for making decisions for the community, you could use one of our other related methods to test the listening process. One, often called meeting for clearness, is for a couple or individual making a decision. Classically, this might be a decision about whether or not to get married. It can also be used for other issues – for someone deciding whether or not to take a job, or have a major surgery, or whatever other questions come up in life. The process is very similar to a meeting for worship for business but the decision rests with the focus individual or couple. Another, often called a threshing meeting, is an opportunity for a whole community to share their knowledge and feelings – about redecorating the bathroom, about how to build peace, or all sorts of other issues – without the pressure to reach a decision at that time.

It would also be possible to use the method to check the method. Find a path to stillness. Get together with some others who also want to know. Look for God's voice speaking within you, and ask: what test should I use? You may hear the Light suggesting an experiment.

Take heed, dear Friends, to the promptings of love and truth in your hearts. Trust them as the leadings of God whose Light shows us our darkness and brings us to new life.
(Britain Yearly Meeting, *Quaker faith & practice*, Advices & Queries 1)

For More Information

Quaker groups around the world list information online. If you want to find out what's happening near you, you can start with the Friends World Committee for Consultation world page: http://fwcc.world/. Remember that in this book I have described the liberal Quaker tradition, and Quaker meetings and Friends churches around the world will vary.

The books produced by Quaker groups, some of which I discussed in detail in the middle of this book, are often available online or through libraries and bookshops. There is a slow but continuous process of change so Internet searches by Yearly Meeting are best. The Library of the Society of Friends, based at Friends House in London, tries to maintain a list which you can download from their website: https://www.quaker.org. uk/resources/library/about-the-collections (in the right hand column under 'subject guides').

Quaker groups discussed in detail in this book are:

- Quakers in Southern Africa: http://www.quakers.co.za/
- Quakers in Britain: http://www.quaker.org.uk
- Quakers in Ireland: https://quakers-in-ireland.ie/

Quakers in Britain will send out a free pack to enquirers, which can be a useful starting point if you are relatively new to understanding Quakers. It can be ordered from their website: https://www.quaker.org.uk/about-quakers/order-a-free-information-pack

Also good for beginners, and often useful for the experienced and knowledgeable as well, are the QuakerSpeak videos produced in the USA by Friends Journal. These short videos come out weekly and the collection covers almost every aspect of Quaker life. Watch them at: https://quakerspeak.com/

Woodbrooke, the Quaker centre where I work, offers courses about all aspects of Quakerism and a selection on other forms of spirituality. This includes courses which can be taken in person or online. There are courses on Quaker worship, Quaker history and theology, meeting for worship for business, aspects of the Quaker business method, and courses for clerks of meetings and people who want to use the methods described in this book. Find full details at: https://www.woodbrooke.org.uk/

Individual Quakers also write numerous books and blogs and articles. I encourage you to explore but want to recommend here just a few which are related to the topics I have covered in this book.

- Craig Barnett, *The Guided Life: Finding Purpose in Troubled Times* (Christian Alternative, 2019)
- J. Brent Bill, *Life Lessons from a Bad Quaker: A Humble Stumble Toward Simplicity and Grace* (Abingdon Press, 2015)
- David Boulton, *Real like the daises or real like I love you?* (Dales Historical Monographs, 2002)
- Nicholas Burton and Jonathan Bainbridge, 'Spiritual Discernment, the Incorporated Organization, and Corporate Law: The Case of Quaker Business Method', published in *Religions,* 2019
- Pink Dandelion, *The Liturgies of Quakerism* (Ashgate Publishing, 2005)
- Jane Mace, *God and decision-making* (Quaker Books, 2011)
- Rachel Muers, *Testimony: Quakerism and Theological Ethics* (SCM Press, 2015)
- Janet Scott, *Towards a Quaker Theology* (Swarthmore Lecture, 1980)
- Gil Skidmore, *Turning Inside Out: an exploration of spiritual autobiography* (Sowle Press, 1996)
- Laura Rediehs, *Quaker Epistemology* (Brill, 2019)

- D. Elton Trueblood, *The Trustworthiness of Religious Experience* (Swarthmore Lecture, 1939)

You are also welcome to contact me directly. I am on social media – on Facebook as Rhiannon Grant, on Twitter @bookgeekrelg – and I write a blog at http://brigidfoxandbuddha.wordpress.com

Also in this series

Quaker Roots and Branches
John Lampen

Quaker Roots and Branches explores what Quakers call their 'testimonies' – the interaction of inspiration, faith and action to bring change in the world. It looks at Quaker concerns around the sustainability of the planet, peace and war, punishment, and music and the arts in the past and today. It stresses the continuity of their witness over three hundred and sixty-five years as well as their openness to change and development.

Telling the Truth about God
Rhiannon Grant

Telling the truth about God without excluding anyone is a challenge to the Quaker community. Drawing on the author's academic research into Quaker uses of religious language and her teaching to Quaker and academic groups, Rhiannon Grant aims to make accessible some key theological and philosophical insights. She explains that Quakers might sound vague but are actually making clear and creative theological claims.

What Do Quakers Believe?
Geoffrey Durham

Geoffrey Durham answers the crucial question 'What do Quakers believe?' clearly, straightforwardly and without jargon. In the process he introduces a unique religious group whose impact and influence in the world is far greater than their numbers suggest. *What Do Quakers Believe?* is a friendly, direct and accessible toe-in-the-water book for readers who have often wondered who these Quakers are, but have never quite found out.

THE NEW OPEN SPACES

Throughout the two thousand years of Christian tradition there have been, and still are, groups and individuals that exist in the margins and upon the edge of faith. But in Christianity's contrapuntal history it has often been these outcasts and pioneers that have forged contemporary orthodoxy out of former radicalism as belief evolves to engage with and encompass the ever-changing social and scientific realities. Real faith lies not in the comfortable certainties of the Orthodox, but somewhere in a half-glimpsed hinterland on the dirt track to Emmaus, where the Death of God meets the Resurrection, where the supernatural Christ meets the historical Jesus, and where the revolution liberates both the oppressed and the oppressors.

Welcome to Christian Alternative... a space at the edge where the light shines through.
If you have enjoyed this book, why not tell other readers by posting a review on your preferred book site.

Recent bestsellers from Christian Alternative are:

Bread Not Stones
The Autobiography of An Eventful Life
Una Kroll
The spiritual autobiography of a truly remarkable woman
and a history of the struggle for ordination in the Church of
England.
Paperback: 978-1-78279-804-0 ebook: 978-1-78279-805-7

The Quaker Way
A Rediscovery
Rex Ambler
Although fairly well known, Quakerism is not well understood.
The purpose of this book is to explain how Quakerism works as
a spiritual practice.
Paperback: 978-1-78099-657-8 ebook: 978-1-78099-658-5

Blue Sky God
The Evolution of Science and Christianity
Don MacGregor
Quantum consciousness, morphic fields and blue-sky
thinking about God and Jesus the Christ.
Paperback: 978-1-84694-937-1 ebook: 978-1-84694-938-8

Celtic Wheel of the Year
Tess Ward
An original and inspiring selection of prayers combining
Christian and Celtic Pagan traditions, and interweaving their
calendars into a single pattern of prayer for every morning
and night of the year.
Paperback: 978-1-90504-795-6

Christian Atheist
Belonging without Believing
Brian Mountford
Christian Atheists don't believe in God but miss him: especially the transcendent beauty of his music, language, ethics, and community.
Paperback: 978-1-84694-439-0 ebook: 978-1-84694-929-6

Compassion Or Apocalypse?
A Comprehensible Guide to the Thoughts of René Girard
James Warren
How René Girard changes the way we think about God and the Bible, and its relevance for our apocalypse-threatened world.
Paperback: 978-1-78279-073-0 ebook: 978-1-78279-072-3

Diary Of A Gay Priest
The Tightrope Walker
Rev. Dr. Malcolm Johnson
Full of anecdotes and amusing stories, but the Church is still a dangerous place for a gay priest.
Paperback: 978-1-78279-002-0 ebook: 978-1-78099-999-9

Do You Need God?
Exploring Different Paths to Spirituality Even For Atheists
Rory J.Q. Barnes
An unbiased guide to the building blocks of spiritual belief.
Paperback: 978-1-78279-380-9 ebook: 978-1-78279-379-3

Readers of ebooks can buy or view any of these bestsellers by clicking on the live link in the title. Most titles are published in paperback and as an ebook. Paperbacks are available in traditional bookshops. Both print and ebook formats are available online.

Find more titles and sign up to our readers' newsletter at
http://www.johnhuntpublishing.com/christianity
Follow us on Facebook at
https://www.facebook.com/ChristianAlternative